THE BATSFORD COLOUR BOOK OF CORNWALL

THE BATSFORD COLOUR BOOK OF
Cornwall

Introduction and commentaries by
Peter Manning

B. T. BATSFORD LTD LONDON

First published 1974

Text © Peter Manning 1974

Filmset by Servis Filmsetting Ltd, Manchester
Printed and bound in Great Britain by William Clowes & Sons Ltd, Beccles, Suffolk
for the publishers B. T. Batsford Ltd, 4 Fitzhardinge Street, London W1H 0AH

ISBN 0 7134 2808 2

Contents

Introduction

The Cornish peninsula, beautiful, insular and unique, a strange combination of holiday playground and private kingdom, is an island in fancy and almost in fact. For 80 miles, its rocky triangle, forging west, thrusts aside both the English Channel and the Atlantic Ocean. A third boundary, to the east, which for all but four miles of hill land, neatly divides it from the rest of England, is the deep slow-moving Tamar River. This mighty stream, the largest of five sparkling rivers where salmon and sea trout run, is the legendary 'Cornish Frontier'. Over it today surge only welcome invaders, but the concept of an actual demarcation line between Cornwall and all foreign parts, including England, is still curiously valid. The history of the Duchy, with its culture and special identity, is intensely shaped by traditions of physical isolation and implacable independence. The Tamar, 57 miles long, is alone the most significant factor of an endemic air of 'separateness' in a promontory that has been penetrated but never conquered. The unbroken legacy of 'dark races speaking strange tongues' makes it one of six surviving Celtic nations, and its name, spoken in the Cornish language as Kernow, means 'Land of Strangers'. It is, however, strangely friendly. The Cornish welcome, based as much on human dignity and respect as on pasties and saffron cake, is as legendary as its frontier.

Physically it is a granite kingdom. Cutting through shales and sandstones to form the gently rounded profiles of its uplands, runs a deep-seated central spine of granite, the crystalline rock of quartz and mica, known locally as Moorstone. From it, come mineral deposits which made Cornwall pre-eminent in production of tin and copper in the last century and, in this, the world's leading producer of china clay. But it is, at the same time, a lush kingdom, rich in wild life. Over its shores swoop cormorants and razor bills, oyster catchers and herring gulls. In clear seas grey seals bark and, shadowing the blue mackerel shoals, sharks patrol the offshore reef. In tall cliffs, ravens live and, though the Cornish chough, with 'its talons and beak all red with blood', an emblem of the county arms through which, says legend, the spirit of King Arthur lives, is sliding to extinction, in woods and meadows the buzzards, kestrels and peregrines hunt unchallenged. On the north downs in October, butterflies, clouded yellows, painted ladies and tortoiseshells, still flutter in peace.

More than 60 places are acknowledged areas of special scientific interest, for Cornwall has more derelict land, virtually irreclaimable, than any other county. Sixteen thousand acres of old quarry sites, abandoned shafts and ruined mine workings, have been called 'the most obstinate, complex and sensational concentration of heaps and holes in these islands', but as a holiday playground the other 852,000 acres coolly justify a reputation as 'The English Riviera'. Almost the whole 400 miles of coastline, from towering cliff to sheltered cove, is classified as possessing outstanding natural beauty. Deeper west, where bog iris and periwinkle give way to camelias and palm trees, terraced gardens are sub-tropical in appearance, inviting direct comparison with the Mediterranean from where its most distinctive colonists are thought to spring. On the north coast surfers glide through white-striped rollers of the Atlantic and in the south, better-known for limpid rock pools and sheltered harbours, skin divers gather crayfish and lobsters from the sea bed. In green tumbling rivers, the Tamar, Lynher, Fowey, Camel and Fal, run silver salmon and the strong fighting sea trout known as peal.

The main ingredients of bewitchment though are classically simple: a shining sun and sparkling seas. The same elements of earth and fire, wind and water, have wrought also, by natural alchemy, a land strong with legend where the giant, authenticity, rides always with dwarfs of folklore and imagination pulling imperiously at the stirrup. Much of Cornwall's chronicle has survived by word of mouth as a semi-private conversation between people holding poetic truth and its promise of ultimate meaning, to be as relevant, and more interesting, than literal truth. A resigning archdeacon, confessing himself unable to communicate with his flock, made a comment 500 years ago which still rings with precision. He said: 'The folk of these parts are quite extraordinary, being of a rebellious temper and obstinate in the face of attempts to teach and correct.' The Romans were in Cornwall for over three centuries but, as hardly a trace of their culture remains, it seems likely that 'a bold rebellious peasantry' finally rid itself of the unwanted outpost of the mighty Roman Empire simply by ignoring it. The bare fact that Cornwall is administratively only one of 53 traditional counties of England and Wales is regarded by loyalists as merely incongruous, but, despite a Nationalist Party dedicated to political independence, and a thriving Mebyon Kernow (Sons of Cornwall) organisation dedicated to preserving and enhancing the Celtic character, Cornwall retains few serious pretensions to nationhood. An economy long based on the uncertainties of agriculture, mining and fishing now includes light industries, mild suburban development and an open attempt to increase the harvest of tourism.

Cornwall, though, is still more of a concept than a county. Where fact and fiction, myth and magic, have blended so long, racial allegiance cuts especially deep. Through a mysterious past flit many well-defined shadows of origin: the long-preserved authority and influence of the Druids, uninhibited fertility rites, love feasts and the worship of strange gods, and many existing customs present vivid reminders of a pre-Christian era. Among elaborate May Day celebrations marking the advent of Spring, the floral dance at Helston, where old men in toppers dance Cornish maids through ribboned streets, is familiar, but the Padstow Hobby Horse, a device of ferocious appearance, glowing eyes and flowing plume, gives a more direct clue to the archaic original. Hurling with a silver ball, which takes place at St Columb, occurs nowhere else in England. Always behind the merrymaking are whispers of primitive statements and rhythms that calmly defy rationalisation. On Midsummer Eve, Old Cornwall Societies, founded in 1920 to prevent a breakdown of ancient patterns and enshrine a Cornish revival of identity, light hill top fires from Land's End to the Tamar, a relic, now purely festive, of ceremonies once red with sacrifice.

The land is still well-equipped with drolls and superstitions, well-stocked with wart charmers, though worship of the sun god is presently limited to rival claims for the highest degree of ultra-violet light, the prime ingredient of a golden tan. Ultra-clarity, a reason why artists find the area so sensuously attractive, results largely from reflections of the sea. No part is more than 15 miles from the coast and most are less than five. In autumn and winter prevailing south-west winds, which on exposed headlands turn knarled blackthorn into starkly pointing fingers, can turn to fierce gales, but spring comes six weeks early and in summer-time, or 'the pleasant days', white clouds sail high and seas lap only gently at their shores.

Three thousand years ago these same shores witnessed arrival of the Celts, a tough dynamic people, tall, blue-eyed and muscular, originating somewhere north of the Alps and speaking the guttural tongue which survives in Gaelic, Erse, Manx, Welsh, Breton and Cornish. Many farmsteads, such as Nancarrow ('Valley of Stags'), bear their original names, as do several Domesday woods such as Dreynes wood near Liskeard or the famed Pencarrow group near Bodmin. On the open moorlands lived survivors of the Bronze Age, and to coastal towns, from the Mediterranean, came the dark, stocky Veneti, intermediaries in the tin trade. Characteristics of the eventual population are an amalgam, with emphasis on the traders in tin. Mining, mainly for tin and copper but also for wolfram, zinc, lead, iron, fluorspar, arsenic and even uranium, is basic to the Cornish. They traded ores with the Phoenicians, who traded the secret of clotted cream in part return. In the twelfth century Cornwall had its own Charter of the Stannaries with private courts designed to keep order and see that tin went first to one of four coinage towns, at Helston, Truro, Lostwithiel and Liskeard, there to be weighed, assayed and stamped with the Duchy Arms. When times were bad there were riots. Men and boys, working frequently for a share of the mine yield known as 'tribute', lived in conditions of grinding toil and dire poverty. In the nineteenth century the average expectation of life of miners in some parts was barely 30. More than 100 mines were once providing two-thirds of the world's copper and the mining industry, directly or indirectly, employed over 100,000 people. In the 1860s, because ores from Malaysia were cheaper, the boom collapsed and production plummeted. By the end of the century, one-third of the mining population had gone. Many emigrated to America and when Dame Fanny Moody, the 'Cornish Nightingale', sang the Song of the Western Men on the South African Rand, it was to thousands of silent exiled Cornishmen. The practical experience and inherited skill of 'Cornish Jack' has contributed to mining endeavours on a large scale and it is still claimed, a little wryly but with pride, that at the bottom of any large hole in the world will be found a Cornishman looking for something.

A current revival of mining, steered by giant companies, makes the individual prospector finally obsolete, though a small echo of his passion for dissidence remains. Every traditionalist in favour of revival has an environmental objector close on his heels. The Cornish, whose special brand of mine-dwelling piskies are known as 'Knockers', live intrinsically close to nature. In consequence their religions, pagan, celtic, orthodox or nonconformist, tend to be passionate and highly personalised. About 1,400 years ago the Saints, mainly from Wales and Ireland and each with a private miraculous legend, came marching in. Hundreds of place names, churches and monuments commemorate their existence and, although no direct information survives, it is plain that these holy men and women, living in monasteries or as hermits, were not fairy-tale characters. The national flag, a white cross on a black field, is that of St Piran, patron saint of the tinners. Christian faith arrived about the fourth century, giving way in the tenth to a constantly disputed union with the English system. Twice the land erupted in actual rebellion. In 1497, with religious feelings deeply involved, one group, armed with picks and crowbars, marched to London demanding to speak to the King and another, which got only to Taunton, stopped first at Bodmin to proclaim Perkin Warbeck as the monarch. In 1549 a rebellious group crossed the Tamar again demanding that the prayer book be printed in Cornish. Expulsion under force of arms by the English, and the consequent penalty of heavy taxes, ingrafted a deep resentment which still, more with magic than logic, bears identifiable trace elements. When

John Wesley, a 'gallant irregular soldier of the Lord', offering total disregard for status and a religious constitution which came down from heaven 'piece by piece as it was wanted', began a triumphal tour in 1743, he found a soil well prepared. Cottage meetings and chapels blossomed and 'Cornish Methodism' gained a special intensity. Billy Bray, a drunken lascivious miner transformed into a pious eccentric, best-known of many homespun evangelists, built a chapel with his own hands and fashioned the pulpit from his bedroom furniture.

Few standpoints, however, in Cornwall, where everything is politely arguable, enjoy unanimity. Wesley objected to smuggling. A large number of his followers, one of whom said the ten commandments were significantly quiet on the matter, did not, for the old time smuggler was a popular folk hero and breadwinner. From the thirteenth century this was an audacious centre of free trade, or 'Fair trade' as the participants put it, and the illegal import of 'brandy for the parson and baccy for the clerk' thrived on a vast scale before being stamped out in the 1850s with some heroic terminal battles. The first preventive boat in the country was stationed at Polperro, which also carved a niche as the birthplace of a freebooter hanged at Execution Dock and of Zephaniah Job, smugglers' banker, stockbroker and financial consultant who, in a final frenzy of success, printed his own private banknotes at Crumpelhorn Mill. Fast sailing luggers, intimate knowledge of a dangerous coastline and a thousand natural hiding places were valuable allies of the moonshiners.

Their record is frank and authentic but the related subject of wrecking raises more questions than answers. Understandably no documentary evidence supports a claim that coast dwellers, both peasantry and gentry, actually lured ships on to rocks for pillage with false or shielded lights but evidence is plentiful that in times of extreme poverty shipwreck survivors were murdered on shore, a distinction commending itself more to apologists than victims. The same hated English laws which forbade smuggling defined a wreck of the sea as anything from which no creature, man or beast, escaped to shore alive. When Sir John Killigrew erected the first Lizard light in 1619, partly in the hope of levying toll on passing ships, local inhabitants were enraged that he should endanger the hereditary right of plunder given by 'God's grace'. A high proportion of houses are still supported on ships timbers. During the 1800s, in the space of just over 20 years, 131 vessels were lost between Land's End and Trevose Head alone, a distance of about 50 miles. At the same time the county has a proud record of life saving at sea, with coasts now well protected by lighthouses, harbour lights, coastguards, lifeboats and strong-swimming surf guards.

Fishing, a less iniquitous and more enduring harvest of the sea, was a bulkhead of the economy until the turn of this century and the Cornish Lugger, a 35-foot carvel-built, wide-beamed, round-bilge boat with a single square lugsail, has carved its memorial in nautical history. In them, fishermen hunted the herring shoals off Scotland, Ireland and France and in 1854 a lugger with a seven-man crew braved hurricanes to reach Australia. At one time over 100 mackerel and pilchard boats were counted in the tiny harbour at Mousehole alone. Pilchards, and also sardines which are yearling pilchards, were supplied salted and smoked by the million to Catholic countries of the Mediterranean who loved them, and to a less impressed Royal Navy, on grounds of economy, who retaliated by nicknaming them 'Mevagissey Ducks'.

The handling of small boats in a fearsome graveyard of shipping calls for rare skills. Sharp outcrops of rock, like the notorious circlet of 'Manacles' where each pinnacle has its own name such as 'The Minstrel' or 'Shark's Tooth', hungrily await the incautious. In other places, blown sand, which has buried numerous churches including that of St Piran, has produced vast dunes, known as 'Towans', with the highest at Perranporth reaching a height of 270 feet. A ridge of sand and gravel across Padstow estuary, site of many shipwrecks, is known simply as 'Doom Bar'. In its heyday the fishing industry was the most dependable part of a trembling economy. Mounts Bay Fleet, a facsimile of that used by the fishermen of Brittany, was declared by an international fisheries exhibition to be the finest in the world, though traditional boatbuilding, which used timber from local estates cut in village saw pits and employed hundreds of men, is now virtually extinct.

Until Brunel built his rail bridge over the Tamar, most fish was sold for local consumption or transported to Bristol by fast sailing smacks, but ironically, when fish and transport facilities were most abundant, the industry collapsed. East Coast trawlermen moved in as the main architects of destruction and clashes with local seamen were so fierce that, at Penzance, they were kept apart by soldiers. The introduction of steam drifters, which could fish rougher waters, and a still unexplained migration of inshore shoals, brought about final collapse, though regattas, the annual water sports of skilled oarsmen whose prime aim, as pilots or traders, was to reach a visiting vessel first, have survived. 'Flash' boats, cockleshell descendants of working gigs, race now for silver cups with the same enthusiasm that their forebears raced for silver coins.

Romance in the past, though realistically more attractive in retrospect, has its proper place. The world's greatest love story, that of Tristan and Isolde, is rooted at Castle D'or, near Fowey, with enough archaeological evidence to provide a reasonable basis of truth, and the little town of Zennor holds dear its legend of the mermaid who lured a chorister beneath the waves so as never again to be parted from his song. Fishermen, whose unaccompanied quayside melodies sound like murmurs of the morning breeze, can still sing like angels. Not all characteristics of a race so classically wild on the wing, of course, are universally endearing. Charges of slyness, hypocrisy, an obsessive love of illness, litigation and argument, have all been levelled in their time. Even haloes are sometimes worn askew and a passion for individuality has bred many characters strong with the beat of blood. Bob Fitzsimmons, the Helston-born champion world heavyweight, proclaimed a great love of fisticuffs by presenting his third wife, on their marriage day, with a portrait of his second. The barefoot art of Cornish wrestling, which once rode a national wave of popularity with immaculate rules of fair play, often descended on its home ground into a free-for-all punch up. In recent years a village battle for possession of the Maypole ended with the use of shotguns, and the last recorded case of cannibalism in England emanated from Falmouth.

'Separateness' from the common weal, however, is normally manifested more gently. Cornish dialect is content to call thistles 'thastles' and brambles 'brimbles', and many a newcomer, greeted softly as he pays toll to cross the Tamar with the guileless phrase, 'Thank you my lover', notes instinctively his arrival at the threshold of a private tongue. In Cornwall a stone wall, packed with earth and supporting a wealth of wild flowers, is a 'hedge'. There is almost private weather, too, for geographic quirks confine extremes to small localities, and, in philosophic terms, there is also a private clock. Time, in a land which still has many worlds to conquer, is not tyrannical. The traditional stoic pursuits of fishing and mining are being replaced by more bustling activities of tourism – in one year the static population of 383,000 is host to three million visitors – but the pace of life remains magically unflurried. Cornwall, where John Harris, miner and poet, said 'the primrose blooms in winter's footprint', proclaims itself, through dignified, silent conviction, as a private kingdom that is not only unique, but spellbound. In all the 150 years existence of Bodmin county jail, no-one ever climbed the granite wall to freedom.

ARRIVAL: THE TAMAR BRIDGE

The 'Gateway to Cornwall', or, since Launceston lays equal claim to the title, the main one. Two bridges, 100 years apart.

In 1859 Isambard Kingdom Brunel, Victorian genius, threw 4,000 tons of cold iron into the curling Royal Albert Rail Bridge, then the first and now the only rail link, and, from his deathbed, heard it called a wonder of the world. In 1961 the Tamar Road toll bridge, privately built by Cornwall and the neighbouring city of Plymouth in an atmosphere of unusual harmony, superseded a ferry service granted by the Black Prince and, like a falling sword, finally made an end of the mighty River Tamar as a traditional and physical frontier.

Where the bridges end, legend begins. Saltash is the oldest borough. From it, 500 years ago, a small sailing ship without chart or compass reached the Arctic Circle and, in its castle, Sir Francis Drake, who married a local fishergirl, stored captured Spanish treasure.

DISPUTED BARRICADES: LAUNCESTON CASTLE

The great castle of Dunheved at Launceston, an early stronghold of the Earl of Cornwall, and later of Cornwall's first Duke, the Black Prince, was used enthusiastically to repel invaders. In fact, like Trematon Castle at Saltash, it was built originally by King William, partly to 'superintend the spirited Cornish'.

On the north coast, dramatic ruins of another 'frontier' castle, King Authur's 'impregnable fortress' from which Tintagel gets its name, has surrendered openly to tourists. King Arthur drove the Saxons away. His successors, untroubled by arguments about authenticity and content in the belief that history holds 'truth enough', welcome them back with enthusiasm to the remains of his clifftop castle and adjoining monastery.

The Arthurian legend is widespread and stubborn. Goss Moor is said to be the King's hunting ground and Camelford, the poet Tennyson's Camelot. Dozmary Pool, a large moorland lake near Bolventor, and Loe Pool, further west, are both claimed as the mere where finally 'flash'd and fell' the jewelled sword Excalibur.

SMALL HARBOURS: BOSCASTLE

On the iron-bound north coast, where Atlantic winds shape natural cathedrals from towering cliffs, small quays provide an especially welcome inner sanctum. Fishing, both professional and amateur, yields a variable harvest in coastal villages with an ageless, simple fascination and in most, the harbour wall is strongly reminiscent of a mother's arm, curved protectively about her child. The sea, both granary and grave-yard, is a quixotic friend but fearsome enemy.

At one time, over 10,000 people were engaged in seine and drift netting, following the 'quick eyed gannet which marks the shoal', and in longlining and crabbing. The industry has eroded, but jagged offshore reefs survive intact. Few fishing grounds are free of some special hazard.

Here, at Boscastle, especially when the herring gulls are stormbound and white horses ride each wave, the inner harbour remains serene. An unusually clear blueprint of the hard practicalities underlying much that is also quaint and picturesque.

THE MYSTIC STONES: TRETHEVY QUOIT

Trethevy Quoit near Liskeard, a burial chamber probably built between 1800 and 1200 B.C., and among the most dramatic of Cornwall's many prehistoric monuments, is one of 13 such quoits.

The eastern area also includes King Doniert's Stone, memorial to a ninth-century Cornish King, and The Hurlers, three sprawling bronze-age stone circles set on open moorland. Legend says they are men petrified for the sin of indulging in the game of Hurling on the Sabbath.

Also near, set high, is the granite Cheesewring, one of many strange rock formations of uncertain origin. Historians believe it was a hill fort; romantics claim Druidical connections and geologists record it as one of many 'rocking stones' where natural erosion has created such delicate balance that the upper stone can sometimes be moved with a pole. Such experiments are doubly hazardous. Each stone enjoys an aura of respect breached only at peril. The Cornish have a terrible fondness for their curiosities.

NATIONAL TRUST: LANHYDROCK HOUSE

Lanhydrock House, a stately home in the valley of the River Fowey, was given by its owner, the seventh Lord Clifden, to the National Trust. This independent charity has wide contrasting interests in Cornwall, ranging from the easy elegance of large estates, lush gardens, parks and woodland, to cottages of more humble appeal.

Unusually picturesque dwellings include fishermen's net lofts, village schools, traditional farm buildings, the engine house of an old copper mine and one, nestling beside Cotehele House, an impressive Tudor mansion of the Edgcumbe family on the River Tamar, known simply as 'Old Stan's Cottage'. Many are preserved through conversion to furnished accommodation for holiday letting.

The Trust has jurisdiction over many miles of coast, about 15,000 acres in all, including headlands, beaches, coves, fishing harbours and coastal farms. Its efforts, allied to those of the Countryside Commission, make it possible to walk freely most of the coastline along well-defined cliff paths which stretch, in all, for 270 miles.

THE GRANITE KINGDOM:
ROUGH TOR AND BODMIN MOOR

Typical of granite outcrops marking the uplands of Bodmin Moor is Rough Tor, a Tor being the simple name for a rocky height. Close to it is Brown Willy, Cornwall's highest point, which rises 1,375 feet above sea level and from which, on clear days, both coasts are visible.

A total of 80,000 acres of moor and marsh, widely spread, provides a fine wildlife haven. Cornwall Naturalists' Trust, formed in 1962 to protect 'an incomparable heritage', has ten nature reserves and 300 places marked with special interest. On unfenced moors, cattle and sheep graze, and bareback riding, for the breaking in of wild moorland ponies, is a traditional skill of the Cornish country boy.

From a high point in the east, at Kit Hill near Callington, the granite spine running centrally through Cornwall and onwards, beneath the sea, to the Isles of Scilly, is clearly seen as the hump backed core of a massive eroded mountain range.

NEW VOYAGER: POLPERRO

The fishing port of Polperro, whose narrow, winding main street lies typically at the foot of a steep rock cleft, was first in Cornwall to accept the most likely ultimate successor to the motor car. Several years ago county planners used the village to pioneer, against initial opposition, a successful scheme of traffic regulation which is expected to become more widely adopted. During summer months motor vehicles are prohibited from entry for any purpose other than access to premises.

In consequence a beautiful village, in imminent danger of being submerged by traffic, has been restored to a pace of life that is peaceful and pedestrian. The horse bus, plying from a large car park on the outskirts, is a practical form of transport towards the quiet harbour.

Polperro was one of the best-known centres of free trade and has a unique museum devoted to the arts of smuggling. It also boasts a famous choir of fishermen.

FIGHTING FOWEY

Once a walled town, Fowey had its status as a cinque port, with harbour jurisdiction stretching from Falmouth to Plymouth, withdrawn almost wholly through a predilection for piracy. When truce was called to wars with the French, a Fowey fleet of 40 privateers, manned by crews of 'thorough going sea pirates' unwilling to surrender rich rights of plunder under the flag of patriotism, carried on the war privately. In return, the French sailed in and sacked the town. Today, by contrast, it exudes an air of almost committed serenity and is a place of quiet pleasures, where only sails tremble in the breeze.

At Pelynt, midway between Fowey and Looe, lies buried Bishop John Trelawney, a hero who was imprisoned in the Tower of London, acquitted and released. His name is immortalised in the characteristically defiant 'Song of the Western Men':

> *Trelawney he's in keep and hold,*
> *Trelawney he may die;*
> *But here's twenty thousand Cornish bold*
> *Will know the reason why!*

CHINA CLAY

Pure white Cornish clay, known as China Clay because the Chinese were first to appreciate its porcelain qualities, consists mainly of the mineral Kaolinite contained in highly decomposed granite. It is outstanding in quality, and quantity. Concentrated at St Austell, mounds of waste quartz and mica sand, from which it is separated, are nicknamed 'The Cornish Alps'.

The clay, once produced by farmers on whose land it was found and later exploited by potters William Cookworthy and Josiah Wedgwood, is now worked exclusively by English China Clays, the largest producing and exporting company in the world. Clay is extracted by water jets and some pits are 400 feet deep, but demand consistently exceeds supply. Deposits, uniquely local, have a life estimated in hundreds of years.

Experiments in reducing waste mounds, which delight artists but irritate conservationists, include the ingenious. With such an abundance of waste sand, several small communities have neatly transformed muddy river banks into 'instant' beaches.

FISHING VILLAGE: MEVAGISSEY

Mevagissey, once a pilchard port of renown, retains a strong, authentic tang of the sea. Its tea shops generate an old-fashioned air of hospitality and its trinkets include shells and sea urchins, locally gathered.

When smuggling was at its height, Mevagissey-built craft, noted for fast sailing qualities, were in demand from Land's End to Dover. Some carried 1,000 yards of canvas in the mainsail and could cross the English Channel in eight hours.

Difficulties of access, allied to a deep tradition of gentle insularity, provide a natural brake against spoliation. It was a Mevagissey man, Walter Cross, who in 1796 set up the first stage coach between the ferry at Torpoint and Truro, but the inhabitants have no tradition of journeying far by land. Their holy well sets the pattern of self-sufficiency. Among hundreds with a specific legendary power of cure, theirs is among few that are good for any ailment.

NEWQUAY

A sophisticated resort developed intensely for tourism, of which 'The Island' is a distinctive feature, Newquay is well-equipped with sport and pleasure gardens, cafes, restaurants, cinemas, a boating lake and an airport. Numerous sandy beaches, with blue and white Atlantic rollers racing shorewards, are ideal for surfing and the area includes many well-known beauty spots. One of them is the superb natural architecture of Bedruthan Steps. On a headland over the harbour, stands a well-preserved 'Huer's House', relic of the ancient craft of spotting fish shoals by the naked eye and of directing the efforts of netsmen by hand and voice from a clifftop.

A modern approach to tourism, more formalised than most, includes lavish provision of hotels and guest houses and for tents and caravans. In summer, even seabirds defer to the calls of tourism. Magnificent black-backed gulls, with a developed taste for cucumber sandwiches equal to that for fresh herring, indulge in spectacular flying displays by the busy promenades.

INNS AND TAVERNS: THE OLD ALBION, CRANTOCK

Many such, like the Old Albion in the village of Crantock, with its walled up smugglers' tunnel to the beach, have a chequered history. This 400-years-old inn, whose doors stayed shut for 72 years because of a temperance revival, may, like the village itself, exist above an earlier community which was overwhelmed by sand when its people 'fell into evil ways'.

Taverns, and private beer houses known as 'Kiddleywinks', where landlords did their own brewing, were once established in every town and hamlet. The only remaining public house carrying on, ceremoniously, the craft of home brewing is the Blue Anchor at Helston where another inn, The Angel, has cemented in its wall, part of the Stone of Hell, a meteorite from which Helston is said to derive its name.

Coaching houses, inns, taverns and beer shops are traditionally popular public meeting places. A whole book was garnered, literally, from bar gossip of the Tinners' Arms at Zennor.

TRURO CATHEDRAL

Truro, which had the first charter granted to a Cornish town, in 1132, and became a city in 1877, is both tranquil and elegant. Bodmin is the more bustling, official county town. Truro, the main centre of county administration, is effectively the capital. In the eighteenth and nineteenth centuries, when many fine mansions were built by landed gentry with wealth based on mining, it was known as the London of Cornwall. Lemon Street is one of the best preserved Georgian streets in England.

With a reputation of being always 'clean, bright and busy', Truro still has many quaint and crooked alleyways wandering idly through its byways. The seductions of serenity, however, are not the only reason it is easier to arrive than to depart. Most of the city lies in a deep bowl and all its exits are uphill.

Its cathedral, consecrated in 1887 and one of the few built in modern times, was raised by the united efforts of all religious denominations.

TRANQUILLITY: HELFORD

An air of undisturbed calm pervades the garden village of Helford for it
is central to an area characterised by tall trees overhanging slow moving
waters. The Helford River itself, on the bed of which, at Port Navas,
thrives a Duchy oyster farm, has a quiet air of indolence and wellbeing.
It ends at the tiny village of Gweek, where silted moorings and deserted
quays are sole remains of the once busy port of Helston, home of the
famous furry dance, of Henry Trengrouse, inventor of the maritime
rocket line thrower, and of Tamson Blight, Cornwall's best-known
witch.

Helford, and the riverside villages surrounding it, cast their own
spell. It is found in the still reflections of Frenchman's Creek, in the
colourful gardens of Glendurgan spilling down a hillside, and in the
quaint village of Manaccan with its thatched inn, bow-fronted shop and
its ancient church, with a fig tree growing from the wall!

ISLAND IN THE SKY: ST MICHAEL'S MOUNT

St Michael's Mount, owned by the National Trust, is considered one of the most attractive sights in Cornwall. Its 70 acres, a mile in circumference, are 231 feet high, with an ancient chapel at the summit reached by winding stairs. At low tide, it can be reached on foot over a narrow causeway of pebbles; at high tide only by boat.

Legend says that St Michael, the county's patron saint, first touched the tip of the mount with his feet when descending from heaven to earth, and in early times it was a place of pilgrimage. As the island of Itkis, it was a main early centre for the export of tin.

For many years, it housed a priory of Benedictine monks, but it has also overlooked some unholy squabbles. The sparkling bay in which it is set, with Penzance and Newlyn nearby, was a popular haunt of swashbuckling pirates and smugglers 'notorious for perjury, drunkenness, idleness, poverty and contempt of the law'.

MINING: ST JUST

Many wastelands are marked by gaunt chimney stacks and crumbling engine houses, memorials of a ruined empire. This one, part of the Botallack workings at St Just, is close to the notorious Levant mine where men worked in candlelight below the sea bed nearly a mile from shore. At Levant, in 1919, a shaft disaster killed 31 men. Eleven years later, the sea burst in and above it, still, the waves run red with escaping ores.

The tradition of mining, with skills passing from father to son in natural apprenticeship, is a tradition of hazard. At East Wheal Rose, a lead mine near Newquay, 39 men and boys were drowned without warning when a cloudburst flooded the workings. Poverty, overcrowding, accident and disease were common, in contrast to some dazzling fortunes made by adventurers and merchant princes, but Cornwall is still a leader of technique. Students from all parts of the world gravitate to the incomparable School of Mines at Camborne.

SHIFTING SANDS: GUNWALLOE

The church at Gunwalloe, once surrounded by a thriving village, and said to have been built by a sailor as a thank offering after shipwreck, has its walls dashed with spray in times of storm. Many churches, including that of St Piran, patron of the tinners, have been completely buried, for although the character of the Cornish coastline is predominantly one of gaunt cliffs, hard crystals of white sand to the north are brushed to mountainous proportions by harsh Atlantic gales. Resulting dunes, known as 'Towans', reach enormous height. At Perranporth, some are 270 feet high.

Sand covers many things. The belief, that a notorious buccaneer buried a vast treasure in the sandbanks of Gunwalloe, was strong enough to merit a grant of treasure trove to one band of fortune hunters, and another tried to salvage in bulk over two tons of gold coin from the hold of a sunken ship in Dollar Cove nearby. Both projects, their foundations literally on shifting sand, collapsed.

ST IVES

An ancient harbour town with narrow cobbled streets and an unsurpassed quality of light, where artists, themselves picturesque, nestle in quiet colonies.

A town of individuals whose early history, beyond the turnpike road, is one of splendid isolation, and dispute. It once thrived jointly as a pilchard port and as an export centre for mineral ores – and miners fought the fishermen. A local ruling forbade the importation of beer because the home product was so good, and another prohibited the 'Shallal', a celebration of 'infernal music' produced by the beating of kettles and tea trays and the shrieking of whistles and horns.

This stormy past gave way, at the start of the century, to an influx of gentle artists, and its prevailing atmosphere is now quiet spoken and calmly reflective. Bernard Leach has a pottery in Stennack Street. The fifteenth-century church has a Madonna and Child by Barbara Hepworth in its Lady Chapel. Peace has long been with St Ives.

SAND AND SEA: PORTHGWARRA

Porthgwarra is one of many picturesque havens where fascinations extend beyond the waterline. Clear waters, blue, green or turquoise according to depth, nourish a marine life that is abundantly rich. The Gulf Stream, continued as the North Atlantic Drift, brings warm waters to both south and north shores and every rock, cave and blowhole below high-water mark has its pattern of mussels, limpets and barnacles. Pools and moist crevices hold jewel anemones and hermit crabs. Many unusual seaweeds, eel grass, caragheen moss and sea thong, abound. In the middle waters thrive sea urchins, corals and the breadcrumb sponge.

In deeper waters visitors include turtles, whales, seals, porpoises and the friendly dolphin. The shark packs, of mako, porbeagles, threshers and the more common blue, which provide worthy adversaries for big game fishermen, roam eight to ten miles offshore, but every rock pool has its darting shadow, usually that of the humble blenny, or shanny, or the shy little shrimp.

SHIPWRECK: THE LIZARD

The Lizard, first home landfall for ships and England's most southerly headland, has a fearsome history of shipwreck. The splendour, scenically unrivalled by day, of a 300-foot-high tableland reaching far out into the open sea, is a formidable navigation hazard in darkness or fog.

On these clifftops, lie many unmarked graves for, until 1808, when an M.P. for Helston achieved legislation providing for Christian burial at parish expense, the common method of disposing of bodies washed ashore, was hasty interment at the nearest summit, 'finder to be sexton'. More than a quarter of the 4,271 lives saved off the Cornish coast by the Royal National Lifeboat Institution, were in jeopardy through the Lizard.

On Goonhilly Downs nearby, whose windswept acres bred a hardy species of working pony named the Goonhilly, and which are notable also for a rich variety of natural plants, stands the distinctive aerial of the Post Office satellite link.

FAMILY OUTING: PORTHALLACK

With high rainfall, a mellow climate and lush, sweet grass, Cornwall is a luxuriant producer of quality milk and butter. A high percentage of its farmers, however, work homesteads of only a few hundred acres in homespun style a whole epoch away from the cold efficiencies of factory farming. Their 'insularity, devoutness and implacable pig-headedness' includes a respect for individual freedom of almost heroic proportions. It is extended, in natural courtesy, to livestock and on this quiet stretch at Porthallack, near Durgan, by the gently flowing Helford river, cattle from nearby fields, eternally curious, sometimes vary their day by spending a casual, ruminative afternoon on the beach.

Expertise in the making of Cornish clotted cream may have been imported originally by the Phoenicians but the special ingredient of local dairy products is directly 'home produced'. Cows give a better yield if, as part of the economy, they are also part of the family.

SERPENTINE: KYNANCE COVE

Part of the scenic splendour of Kynance Cove is attributable to deposits of Serpentine, a soft rock delicately veined in reds, greens and yellows, which is sometimes veined, in turn, by soapstone. Numerous small quarries and pits support a local industry devoted to the shaping of it, once into pillars, overmantels and tables, now mainly into small ornaments.

Rock formations of the Lizard, which enfolds this cove, are entirely different in character from the rest of Cornwall. Their complexity confounds geologists but their size and colour are a constant delight to the eye tutored only for beauty.

Although cliffs are sometimes used for organised climbing expeditions, such unspoilt and undeveloped stretches of seascape, part of the longest coastline of any English county, are jealously preserved. Kynance, studded with rocks of monolithic size, caverns and small island clusters, inhabited only by seabirds, has a special majesty which many claim has even greater visual impact than Land's End.

LAMORNA

Dreams of a cottage by the sea, desert island remoteness and fresh cool water combine in the cove of Lamorna. It lies at the foot of a deep wooded valley, beside a fast-flowing stream, and for most of the time only echoing cliffs and wild flowers hear the lonely cry of the curlew.

Around it, life has been, and is, bustling and busy. In a nearby hamlet, King Arthur is said to have fought his last battle. To the east is Mousehole, once sacked and virtually destroyed by raiding Spaniards, the fishing port of Newlyn and the breezy town of Penzance, custodian of Cornwall's only promenade. Also close by, stands a Bronze Age stone circle, known as 'The Merry Maidens', legendary memorial to 19 naughty maids petrified for the sin of making merry on a Sunday.

In the still centre, with memories only of a long-abandoned trade in shipping local stone, Lamorna has long been an oasis of solitude, and peace.

LAND'S END

Beyond it lies only the legendary lost land of Lyonesse and a lonely sentinel, the Longships lighthouse. The reef, rising 60 feet at a distance of one and a half miles from shore, was named 'Longships' because in silhouette, particularly at sunset, its line of rocks looks like the passing of a ghostly fleet.

The imagery is apt. Land's End, pounded by tide races, harsh Atlantic winds and the endless turmoil of opposing seas, has seen many ships to their grave. Sixteen miles due west lie the Seven Stones, which in 1967 claimed the Torrey Canyon. Clear, wholesome seas of the county, which nourish marine life in abundance, are only selectively benevolent to man. Trinity House has 15 lighthouses, four automatic, and a light vessel guarding Cornish coasts.

Land's End, the last outcrop of a granite kingdom, holds a fascination beyond the visual impact of its strength and grandeur. It is a place almost of pilgrimage; the westernmost extremity of Britain, majestically silent.